Other Books

Poetry on my Mind
The Fundraising Resource Manual
The Lansing Doctors Directory

CASUAL GARDENING

TOM TENBRUNSEL

CASUAL GARDENING

Cover Photo by Erin Secretarski

iUniverse books may be ordered through booksellers or by contacting:

iUniverse
1663 Liberty Drive
Bloomington, IN 47403
www.iuniverse.com
1-800-Authors (1-800-288-4677)

ISBN: 978-1-6632-0516-2 (sc)
ISBN: 978-1-6632-0517-9 (e)

Print information available on the last page.

iUniverse rev. date: 07/17/2020

"Don't Rush Mother Nature"

For my grandchildren

CONTENTS

FOREWORD

I have jotted down my thoughts and ramblings from my gardening experience over my decades. Where did I learn it? My daddy was a gardener, a Victory Gardener. I have fond memories of that sweet old man, Dad: gardening, baseball (I write right and think right but bat lefty because he said, "the wall's closer in right field"), men's group at Holy Name Church, Boy Scouts, Gillette Friday Night Fights on the old almond-shaped Philco radio, fishing with "hosweed" worms, stalking brim, him giving me the freedom to be myself. The older I get, the more like Dad I get, and that ain't half bad cause people loved my Dad. Mom was my confidant and therapist, which is why I suppose I became a psychologist. Mom played the piano by ear; so do I. So do my grandkids. Dad was common sense. Mom was the family glue.

Me and My Daddy

"If you plant them, they will grow." Gardening is a mere offshoot of nature, an afterthought if you will. Nature and plants and edibles have been around since the beginning. Man then came along and made a few modifications and started planting in rows and pots and plots and acres and hectors. It may seem near impossible to some, but if you plant it, it will grow. So go out and plant it. Which would you rather have a lawn and a grocery store or a garden. Grocery stores are set up to supply food for about two days. Yep, you guessed it. The grid goes down and you have two days. You got a garden, you live year round. And you know what you're eating.

Victory Gardener

I love gardening and have a garden every year. There are endless techniques for home gardening. I have included a bunch of them, just enough to get you started or learn something you haven't thought of yet. I kind of prefer casual gardening (That's why I like my secret garden most). You know, if you plant it, it will grow. I've tried a lot of different types and tips and tricks. It really boils down to what YOU want and that's been my approach in this book. If you have any doubt whether you can garden, grow your own vegetables, just do it. Just get some seeds and plant them. Mother Nature is on your side. Go out and plant it. It will grow.

There's so much to gardening and yet so little. I prefer to garden leisurely, sitting in my garden chair with my sweet tea, watching it grow. The darn plants know exactly what to do. "Just give them a happy home," my dad would say, "And they'll do the rest."

You'll find I use natural means of feeding and caring for plants and protecting them from pests and animals. "Don't need no fancy chemicals." My definition of organic is use Nature. She's pretty savvy. "Got thrip? You gotta get aphids." And you will need a good habitat for lady bugs to eat the aphids. Bees and butterflies to pollinate. You want birds to eat your tomato worms. You'll want your neighbor's cat to hunt varmints. And of course a dog to keep the bears and deer shoed away from your garden.

Most of what I've jotted down for you is lessons learned along the way. It's not complete by any means, but enough to get you started and add a trick or two you may not have heard of. Of course, I'm happy to get advice from others too, so write to me about your experiences growing your own food. I'd welcome hearing from you. Join my Facebook page.

Many blessings upon you for tending the soil. Enjoy!

Tom Tenbrunsel
Weaverville, a'ways out in the country, a might near off the grid, but still real close to those grand babies. We come here to these Appalachian mountains by way of eight states. We like it here and so do my plants.

Let me hear from you.

Follow me on Facebook: TOM TENBRUNSEL AUTHOR

"If you plant it; it will grow."

Supplies You Will Need for the Casual Garden

It certainly depends on what kinda garden you want, but here's a good list:

1. Shovel with hand handle
2. Your grandfather's grub hoe
3. Rake (a small rake for small gardens)
4. Trowel and a Dibber
5. Foam knee pad and a bulb planter
6. A yard wagon or wheelbarrow
7. Nylon trellis netting with large 5" squares
8. Oak or 2x2x8 tomato stakes or baskets
9. 2x12x8 lumber, screws, drill, galvanized corner brackets for raised garden and 1 yard of "Amy's Mix"
10. OR cardboard and straw bales for a Ruth Stout no-dig, no-watering, instant garden
11. Worm buckets
12. Seeds and a garden store
13. Mulch, compose, grass clippings, straw to keep weeds out

VICTORY GARDENING

My happy assistant, Annie, by the Secret Garden

I'm writing this book because my friend Krispian and my grandsons, Nick and Tommy, asked me to put down some of my ideas on gardening. It all started with me and my Dad's Victory Garden a'ways back in the early 1940s. You see, I'm old, but not too old to get out in the garden and putz around. The Nation was engaged in WWII and all food resources were going overseas to feed our troops. We were busy saving France and Europe for the second time against Germany. Every able family was encouraged to grow whatever they could in whatever space they could. People grew what they could on any and every plot of dirt, even if it was in the front yard or on the roofs in the cities. Our family turned a ½ acre into a Victory Garden, growing multiple crops: corn, beans, potatoes, carrots, radish, lettuce, cabbage, broccoli, Brussel sprouts, okra, greens, turnips, beets, tomatoes, peppers, onions, squash, zucchini, asparagus, rhubarb, to name a bunch. We cultivated our side lot, seeded, watered, tended, debugged, harvested, cooked, canned and stored, and shared vegetables with friends and neighbors. We also raised chickens for eggs and meat and rabbits and bees. It was good times. It was a time for pulling together against a common enemy. It was a time of patriotism. It was a time for families and the time I learned to love gardening. I have planted a Victory Garden every year since, nye on 75 years now.

But first a story. 'Bear" with me a moment before we get into gardening per se. Someone once asked me do I carry in my garden? Does a bear . . . In the woods? I live way out up a mountain, sort of off the grid somewhere in Western North Carolina. We are a tad self-sufficient, except for yoga classes at the Y in town, gas for the vehicles and "Brisket Day" at Moe's Original Barbecue. I see wildlife every day. Well, I should carry cause while bears don't bother people for the most part, cougars do. Not the middle-aged married type. I mean wild cougars, I mean the cantankerous mountain lion type. You see bobcats don't growl. A cougar will. Although pretty much invisible most of the time, they get bolder when hunting. A bear will give you a couple a territorial huffs. Those kitty critters can sneak up on you. Hungry, they can get feisty wit' my dog, I swing a mean rake at the pesky rabbits and know some Tea-kwon-Hoe, enough, that is to beat a mean path to the back door. Been false charged before by a big male black bear once up on Rocky Top - messed my pants! So's just in case, I carry, to ward off the pussycat. Momma bear knows me.

I'll cover it later but there are so many tricks to keep the critters large and small outta your garden. I don't fence my garden. Believe it or not a small chunk of Irish Spring placed at each corner of my garden boxes, staves off most everything (even deer) but not the good insects, the birds and the bees and butterflies. I free range a lot of my fruits and veggies and I'll introduce you to my secret garden idea below. Bottom line is you gotta share. If a momma deer nips off every young zucchini start, well, just plant some more. Lord, they are beautiful creatures!

So let's garden together. Using my rules of (green) thumb, you can grow a few choice fresh veggies or sustain your family off the grid. Same techniques work for either or both. I like to think that gardening is a lost skill, easily recovered and really kind of fun. My philosophy is to keep it simple and natural - Put a seed in the ground and it will grow! That-a-way, you can spend as much time as you like gardening. It's healthy, mentally, physically and spiritually. It's like in the olden days when the mentally ill were in hospitals, only we called it occupational therapy gardening back then, sixty years back or so. Or check out that new Clint Eastwood movie, "The Mule," where he ends up gardening and doesn't "let the old man in." That's me.

Well, by no means are my ideas that original, they are garnered from my dad, old timers, from personal experience and preserved here for you to carry-on forward. That's why I put pen to paper, so as to give Tanya, Special K, Ester, and the grandkids a little guidance in the ways I've found work best for me. Like my friend, JD, used to sing, "Thar ain't nuttin' like fried green tomatoes" right outta thu garden. God love you, John, I wish you'd a-left flying experimental planes to the test pilots. Even my plants like "Whispering Jessie."

Anyways, let's talk gardening by saying you can grow anything, anywhere, in any type garden; so do what you want - Casual Gardening. I've done both flat gardening, long straight Victory Garden rows, patches and pots and raised boxes stair stepped down the side of the hill, towers and straw bales and such. I like 'em all, but tend to favor gardening in 4x8 foot raised beds - I call them "postage stamp gardens". Six 4x8 foot raised boxes crammed full-a goodies will feed a couple and a couple o' neighbors and then some. I am leaning toward Rick Austin's "Secret Garden" technique, where he plants stuff like they are used to growing – not in rows but spread about, bunched together here and there. Kinda like they grew in the wild. I was raised a bit OCD, and rows suit me and probably you and most folks. But people who shouldn't, sure as heck couldn't find Rick's garden, even if they were walking right through it. And stealth gardening can come in mighty handy in a pinch of times. So I say spread a few choice veggies around in your flower gardens, folks. Hide them here and yonder in plain sight. And think of a greenhouse, attached to your house, heating your house in winter and providing hot water and food all year round. That of course ain't so casual.

There is little rhyme nor reason to Rick's Secret Garden, just plant all over and anywhere, and turn your ducks loose in it to scarf up the bugs and beetles. But for now let's concentrate on how to grow things in boxes and up trellis and poles and towers in a small place with mulch to keep the weeds down and the moisture in, and compost to keep the soil rich without chemical fertilizers. Pick off them bug varmints and feed 'em to the chickens.

3

Planting Zones

The first rule of gardening is to know what planting zone you live in. That is to say what are the weather conditions, sun, wind, rain, moisture, humidity and soil conditions in your area. The US Department of Agriculture and other countries have summarized all this for you by zones. What and when to plant varies by zone. You want to be sure that what you plant can grow and survive by seasons, year round. You can find the characteristics of your zone practically anywhere, especially in catalogs and online. Generally speaking if you purchase plants or seeds locally, they will be right for your zone. All other gardening techniques and tips remain the same from zone to zone.

Another very unique and yearly guide to all things and gardening is The Old Farmer's Almanac. If you have never seen one, buy one at the check out in almost every store. It has been around forever and is full of fun tips. I am not sure whether the "old" refers to the publication, or to old farmers like me!

I think it was Bobby Darin that sang, "Planting is the name of the game; and each generation plants the same," or something to that effect.

LET'S GET TO GARDENING

What will you need? Wood to make the boxes (treated wood works, cause it no longer contains arsenic), "Amy's Mix" (about a yard per raised bed) from a local supplier (or any good rich dirt, a scoop of sandy loam mixed in and compost) and seeds (heirloom seeds trump hybrids, cause next year's crop may depend on the seeds you saved this year). You'll

"Boxes!"

need a source of water to supplement Mother Nature from time to time, especially up here on "dry ridge" as the Reems Creek American Indians named it. Plants require regular watering (though good mulch and some secret straw will help immensely. Good compost content can serve as a way to break down nutrients in the soil so the plants and trees can use them). Then again, I'm gonna cover later how to make a no dig, no water raised box garden.

Oh, and break out that garden rake, hoe, shovel and handmade shovel handled "dibber" that grandpa left for you. I just love my daddy's grub hoe. And you'll need some buckets, a wagon or wheelbarrow and assorted other garden implements. They will come in mighty handy! If you are turning up new ground a rear-tined Troy-Built tiller will be a blessing. You can rent or borrow one, because you won't need it more than once, provided you mix in some good compost and manure that first time. Yes, some seasoned cow or chicken stuff will do the trick! I trade big ripe tomatoes for bantam poop and eggs, with my chicken-raising neighbor down the street. Or just try the Ruth Stout no-dig, no-watering method that I describe below. You got a creek or pond or well? Perfect! Catch your rainwater. City water'll do just fine, except it could dry up in hard times? And get a solar kit for the well pump.

Diversify your crops and species to hedge your bet against a particular crop failing that year. Now enjoy yourself neighbor. Let's get started.

HOW TO MAKE A GARDEN

1. Location, Location, Location! Check your spot for drainage and position of the summer and winter sun

2. Dimensions: I like 4x8' screwed together.

3. Materials: three 2x12x8' per box, eight 3" steel lag-locks, four galvanized corner brackets and deck screws.

4. Assembly: Assemble the box on site preferably as its pretty darn heavy. Make sure you level the placement spot.

4x8x8' raised beds with cardboard underneath, then rough mulch topped off with "Amy's Mix" mixed with sandy loam and straw and grass clippings for top mulch

5. Fill: Cardboard on the bottom, plus "Amy's Mix" plus sandy loam. It takes about a yard per box.

6. Planting: I use a dibber that my daddy made me outta an old shovel handle to poke holes for plants. Mine is tapered with marks every inch. Mulch: Straw and grass clippings and stuff

7. Watering: A sprinkler works OK but a drip system would be nice. I water once every 3 days for 30 minutes just as the sun comes up and shut the system off for rain delay. My sprinkler covers all 7 boxes and the potato towers. My Core raised gardens and my Ruth Stout Garden don't need watering.

8. Fertilizer: Worm castings, cured chicken manure, and epsom salt.

9. Wintering Over: cover my boxes with 12" of straw. Old straw is cheap. Some farmers want you to haul old straw out.

10. Select one of your boxes as a perennial box for asparagus, rhubarb and the like.
11. Hugelkulture Garden: metal oblong bottomless galvanized tub, raised, fill with logs and leaves, then compost, soil, mulch.
12. Ruth Stout Garden: no dig, no watering, no weeds, straw, then add straw as mulch as needed.

SOILS AND ROTATION

Don't! Don't bother to rotate your crops.* Instead, rotate your soil, by adding a 3" layer of good cured compost (soil) on top. It's a great way to recycle. Start with a good quality soil. Andy's Mix plus sandy loam and add compost. As I mentioned, a 4x8' raised bed takes about one yard of soil mix. Then add to it over the years. Add compost, grass clippings, straw. I even mix in perlite and old rotten straw in my beds to soften and hold moisture where I grow carrots, potatoes, turnips, ginger, garlic and the like, that grow under the soil.

Migardner has a great video on why you don't need to rotate your crops in a small garden https://youtu.be/ki2Xc8s44sI

*I think because tomatoes are so prone to carrying over disease and parasites, that I'd collect and remove the vines and leaves and dispose them separately in those city brush pile bags or just burn them if you can in your location, then spread the ashes back on the garden. Don't add them to your compost.

COMPOST BINS

I use a dual compost bin made out of old pallets (free from Loews). Dual because you need a new and an old compartment (Migardner has a great video on how to build a dual compost bin https://youtu.be/wJ0qDEBwkZE). The dual bin has two sides of two pallets, end to end, with one pallet separating them and is open at the top. The dual compost bin is open at each end.

Another very neat self-contained neighborly option are those prefab plastic compost bins sold at local farm stores or on Amazon.

It takes about 5 weeks to cure compost. So while one is done, spread it on your garden. It will keep weeds down and create valuable organic bacteria to make it easier for plants and fruit trees absorb nutrients in the soil. Meanwhile you are adding new clippings plants, weeds, etc. to your new bin. Be sure to leave a few handful of the old compost as a "starter" for the new compost batch. Voila! Recycling complete and you've rotated (added nutrients to) your soil and no crop rotation needed!

Check out Migardener's six steps to successful composting:

1. Leave a couple hand-full-size of old compost as "starter" for new compost.
2. Compost pile should have large surface area (3 by 3 foot is ideal) to let in O2. Keep pieces small for best results.
3. Fork it! Flip (mix) a composting pile several times to get more O2 into it. This will speed up composting and keep the "stink" away.

4. Water to keep it damp
5. Repeat steps 2-4
6. Allow pile to sit and rest and cool for a couple weeks till the worms and ball-bugs come in. Then it's ready.

WORM BEDS

Red wigglers and night crawlers fed with soggy shredded newspaper. And kitchen scraps

Let your worms do all the tilling, aeration, fertilizing, while you relax in the shade in your Adirondack, sipping sweet tea. Ahhhhhhh! Gardening is so darn easy.

I have a bucket-worm-bed in the center of each of my raised beds. Of course worms will seek out good composted soil, but having a 3 gallon bucket with large enough holes under the soil line and on the bottom is a convenient garbage disposal for the house scraps. Believe it or not, worms like shredded newspaper. They gobble up about anything, then go poop in your garden. It's just that simple. No meat or citrus please.

I make my worm buckets out of frosting buckets from the supermarkets. Most of the time they are free for the asking. I drill ⅜ holes all around below the soil line and bottom so the worms can come and eat and go back out to aerate and poop. Worm castings are the best natural fertilizer. Drill smaller ¼ holes in the top to let the rain water in. Just remember to keep those buckets full up, cause worms are ferocious garbage eaters. Keep the lid snapped on the buckets to keep pests out.

You can get your worms where you by bait. I prefer the red wigglers and night crawlers. I carton per worm bed will get you started and be enough to dig out for when you take the grandkids fishing.

13

Looking for night crawlers? Well, they come out and lay on top of lawn at night, hence the name. Stick a pitchfork in the ground and tap on it with a stick and watch your lawn worms come out of hiding. Or you can go out on the sidewalk and gather "boocoos" of worms on a rainy day. They just naturally gravitate to a Ruth Stout straw garden.

DIFFERENT TYPES OF GARDENS

This section covers some of the different types of gardens. Raised Beds, Core Garden*, Straw Bale Garden*, Ruth Stout Garden*, Hugelkulture Garden, Rick's Secret Garden, Traditional Garden, Pot Gardening. Conformity is not the object here. Plant your style or mix and match. Each has an application. My goal is to creat a healthy, renewable garden which is pest free and does not require a lot of maintenance or watering. The gardens listed above that don't require watering are marked with an asterisk.

Traditional Garden

The traditional is just that. It's the garden used by most people over the centuries that families have tended as their vegetable gardens. Traditional gardens are usually in rows and usually worked by tilling, spading or forking the soil. It works, folks. Proof positive. Tilling controls weeds, but weeds grow in tilled soil. What? Well, tilling makes it easy to plant, but attracts weeds. So continued tilling is necessary to keep weeds in check. My dad used to spade and dig his entire garden every Spring. Whew, that's work! He would hitch up mom to the one steel-wheeled hand plow and give her a "Giddy up! Haw!" And off they're go, row by row. Wonder how that turned out? They were enthusiastic Victory Gardeners. I really don't recommend that method of tilling.

After spading, plowing or tilling, and smoothing out with the backside of a garden rake, in a traditional garden make a trench line using twine stretched lengthwise between two stakes to guide the corner of your hoe to make a trench row. I remembering helping my dad move the twine line over to the next row. Sow your seeds. Cover 'em up. And water them in. If you plant them, they will grow.

Folks, having gardened with my dad, in a traditional garden in the heat of the south, barefoot with only shorts on, with sweat lines down my sun-browned back, skinny-assed little boy legs and belly, I prefer a low maintenance garden! I prefer not to disturb the soil if it's good soil. I like a low maintenance garden. Plant in well composted soil, add straw or grass-clippings to eliminate weeds, retain moisture and provide natural bacteria to help plant roots work best. Thar's no need to water. Jest sit back in your garden chair in the shade and nap. Then pick the fruits of little labor and go inside and ate 'em!

I even let my worms do my composting.

Raised Beds - Grow Straight Up to Save Garden Space and Potato Towers

When I taught in the College of Urban Development at Michigan State University, we experimented in those days (the seventies) with "postage stamp" gardens - grow as much as you can in a small space. Feed it with rich compost. "Close gardening" controls weeds too. Those gardens fit well in raised boxes, on top of buildings and places limited only by your imagination. The idea originated from Victory Gardens. The challenge is to produce as much as possible in a small space. I like to think postage stamp gardening may just stave off a cold spell or two in the solar winter the farmers are talking about these days in the 2020s.

Stakes, Trellis and Cattle Panels

Growing straight up is perhaps the best way to make use of garden space. I like to stake tomatoes. But 8 foot oak garden stakes are hard to find these days. 2x2s work great but pull them out after the season and stack them so they don't warp.

Trellis are abundant. You can buy them or fashion your own. I like the nylon trellis net you can find most places. Just throw it over a high horizontal pole and anchor it and your done. By widening it at the base, you can grow on all sides. Mix and match different plants (beans, tomatoes, cucumbers, squash tomatillos) on the same trellis. Cattle Panels are an attractive and handy way to trellis, over or between raised gardens. Cattle panel come in 4x16 foot and now 4x8 foot sizes. Get the 4x8 and bend it over and zip tie the ends together three to a bundle and it will fit neatly into your van or SUV. The use of the 4x8 size is endless in bending over and anchoring to a 4 foot raised bed for a low trellis. Add a plastic cover zip-tied to it and it doubles as a hot bed for early planting or extending growing into the fall. Then, it can easily swing open and be attached to the panel in the adjacent bed to form a high trellis over the walkway - Voila!

Here are some straight up suggestions for raised beds:

1. **Stake Tomatoes** and tie them up the 2x2x8' firmly staked into the ground. I plant 4 tomatoes to a stake which gives me 16 plants per one row along the 8' side of my raised bed. My indeterminate grape tomatoes grow 12 foot tall, so I stake them and let them run across the bean netting when they get too tall to reach. If you got the room let them run on top of a good healthy amount of straw mulch, especially determinant varieties. Plant those delicious grape Tami-G tomatoes, one plant at the end of each pole bean trellis. Let those yummy beauties run with the beans. They like each other. I get around 300 grape tomatoes per plant. Not all my veggies make it into the house. I like to munch-a-lunch in my garden☺

2. **Plant Pole Beans, Peas and Limas.** Get some 3.5x3.5" trellis netting at local garden center and throw over a staked up 2x2, so's you can get double use up either side. I prefer the Golden Gate Romano Pole Beans. They are a heavy producer and as tender as can be, even up to 12" long with no strings attached.

Prolific Potato Towers

17

3. **Trellis your cucumbers.** Keep them heavily mulched to retain moisture. Pick frequently and small for an abundant crop. You can trellis a bunch of things to make room in your garden and to make it easy to harvest. Also, run a couple cucumber plants up your bean poles. And toss a few cukes, or tomatillos on top your potato towers.

4. I have had good luck with **potato towers** made out of either an 8 foot cattle panel or 5 foot hog fencing. With make a nice 3 foot diameter tower. Wire or zip-tie the tower to a t-pole (metal fence post) to keep it upright. I alternate about four 1 foot layers of compost and straw (the more rotten the better). The straw in the tower will hold stuff from falling out. I plant the seed potatoes out 3 to 4 inches from the outer sides, so the plant can go to sunlight out the side and the tubers hang out in the straw. Prepare seed potatoes by cutting in half or leaving two eyes per piece. Leave the cut potato pieces overnight on a cookie tray to harden off the cut sides. Plant about 6 seed potatoes per layer. If you have some old rotten straw you don't need any dirt in your layers. If you don't have some dark rotten straw, SOAK EACH LAYER good as you build up your potato tower. After that, the rain should take care of watering. Think of straw a a sponge and compost! If you used hog wire instead of cattle panel, I cut arm holes alternated around the hog wire for planting and harvesting. Wear gloves and a long sleeved sweatshirt so's you don't scratch yourself up, reaching in. Sometimes I just knock the tower over for a quicker harvest. Reach in and grab a few new potatoes during the growing season - yummy.

5. I like to bend a 4x8 cattle panel in an archway either over my 4x8 raised beds or between beds. Then run cukes up it. They climb up and hang through nicely through the wire for easy pickin's. Summer squash the same. You can even have a picnic lunch on the ground underneath the shaded cuke arch.

6. You might consider short staking other plants like peppers, dill, Brussel Sprouts, asparagus and the like. And I always pinch my bell peppers way back a couple pinches when I plant them, so's they give a bunch a'more fruit.

7. Oh, and get some orchard netting over those blueberry bushes, cause birds have a knack O' spottin' exactly the day when the berries git ripe! And bears can smell over ripe berries a mile away.

Core Garden

A Core Garden is a raised bed garden with a rotted straw core running down the middle underneath the soil. The basic core garden is four feet wide with a 10" wide core dug down in the middle, as long as you want it. The middle trench is filled with 8" of packed rotten straw, then covered with soil. Use straw, mulch or grass-clippings as a top dressing to keep weeds down. Mound up the core and add more soil as the straw deteriorates. It is generally effective for three years, then redo the core with more rotten straw. Worms love it. The straw acts like a sponge to hold rain and moisture, wicking out into the surrounding soil. This type of garden does not require watering.

Straw Bale Garden

This type Garden is very flexible to layout and placement of the bales, cut-side up works fine. Leave the twine on the bale. Set the bales with a cut side up to absorb rain better. Use your imagination as to where you want to place the bales. Keep sunlight in mind. Rotten bales are preferred. You can often find them on farms or at least set them out in the fall to let them cure. Plant on all sides as you wish. Use your dibber to poke holes in the bale for planting on all sides. If the bales are new, give them a good soaking at first. They then won't need watering, because remember straw is like a sponge and soaks up rain. Rotten straw also attracts worms. Good job. Perfect! Keep planting in your straw bale right through till when it turns to dirt. Just add more straw bales next year to expand your garden, then sit back in that old wooden Adirondack easy chair, with some homemade lemon aid and watch your garden grow.

RUTH STOUT NO-DIG, NO-WATERING GARDENING METHOD

1. Pick out a spot anywhere and lay cardboard right out on top of the grass or soil (no digging required).
2. Make it any size that suits you.
3. Spread a generous amount of straw (or hay) about 14" deep, preferably the fall before, so as to let the straw a sit and rest and decompose over the winter.

My Ruth Stout no-dig potato patch!

4. Spread straw to plant potatoes, yams, melons, winter squash, corn, just about anything. Plant garlic and onions and a few marigolds around the perimeter to ward off pests. A little catnip will assure your cat rids those pesky mice and voles.
5. You can sometimes get two seasons.
6. Plant onions and garlic around your plot to fend off all pests. Drop a few cut up cubes of Irish Spring soap around the perimeter.
7. Add more straw as needed for a healthy compost/mulch all season.
8. No need to water as the rotting straw acts like a sponge underneath. If you don't believe me put your hand down to the bottom of 14" of straw mulch. Wet ain't it!
9. When time to harvest, jess pull the straw back and harvest - no need to dig.

10. Add more straw as needed for the winter. The older the garden, the richer the compost effect. I have found that a layer of compost under the straw works best until the Ruth Stout garden has matured over a couple years. By then the rotten straw or hay will have formed a nice compost layer.

11. Add a bunch more straw on top in the fall.

VARIATION RUTH STOUT FOR A SMALL TOMATO GARDEN

Use the backside of your granddaddy's hoe (handed down to you) or the handle of a garden trowel for poking a hole to plant your tomatoes. That-aways after your cardboard's down 2x8' with a 6" mixture of cow manure and dirt on top, and 18" of straw on top of that, you can to plant your six or so (better boy, big boy, Tami-G grape) tomato plants and a couple peppers. You can just poke a 45 degrees slanted hole (plant your tomatoes sort of horizontal down through your seasoned garden straw into the dirt bed and stick the plants from Lowes ¾ ways into the hole. You can water them thoroughly when planting. You can stake indeterminate (tomatoes with one stalk) let the determinate varieties sprawl low profiled but keep them on the straw, mulching under the vines with new straw occasionally. No need for a border on the garden unless you want to. If I were you, I would "sucker" the shoots that appear along the vines to encourage bigger maters.

You won't have to fertilize, but once every 2 weeks crush 1 Tums and 1 aspirin into a liter hand held sprayer from Loews and spray plants liberally. Remember to buy 2 bananas and cut in half and bury the halves shallow horizontally sort of on top where the roots are growing horizontally between the tomato plants. Each banana half (leave peel on) will attract handful of earthworms.

Now buy a two pack of Irish Spring bath soap, cut it into 1/2 inch cubes and place on the corners of your garden box to keep ALL pests away. If that don't work, surround the garden plot with a 12 gauge trip wire☺

No need to water. Unless you get a nasty Oklahoma dust bowl drought. To decide if the small plot needs water, run your hand down into the bottom of the straw. I told you - Like a sponge ain't it and wormy! And, if you didn't lay out your small plot garden last fall, get going early between spring showers!

HUGELKULTURE GARDEN

The most popular Hugelkulture Garden is a three foot metal, oblong, bottomless galvanized tubs, filled on the bottom with logs, then compost, soil and mulch. Some people like the idea of a raised, raised garden. I suppose I'll give it a try when I can't bend over and kneel alongside my boxes. It does look a might handy to work standing and the deep mulch makes a real natural-like base underneath for compost, moisture and good drainage. Those bottomless round or oblong metal frames are at your local farm supply store. Kindly keeps small varmints out but are deer grazing height.

Another way to look at Hugelkulture Gardens is to just gather up all the debris, logs and stuff laying around and dump it in and fill dirt over it. There (dusting my hands together) Done!

RICK'S SECRET GARDEN

Well, I got this idea on how to grow secret stuff in plain sight, from Rick Austin (Just buy his book, *The Secret Garden of Survival*, and any other book by Rick, online). Rick's philosophy is that nature doesn't grow stuff in rows so why should we. Learn what plants like each other and plant them in clumps and bunches all around your place. Sweet potatoes make great ground cover for a flower garden out front and come fall just yank up a mess o' yams. Red cabbage enhances any flower garden. Herbs keep out bugs so spread these fun smelling, tasty plants all over. You can hide bush beans and peas all over too. Rhubarb is a nice perennial to enhance your landscape. Chives and herbs even red cabbage, beets, carrots, colorful small pepper plants, chards and eatable flowers adorn my secret garden. You would never guess there are butternut squash weaving amongst my iris. I even hide a tomato plant or two at ground level. My guests walk right by it every day. Plant some catnip for the neighbors cats to come by on daily patrol, a-looking for a vole, mouse or mole. Sprinkle some Irish Spring chips around your plants if the rodent rascals or deer frequent your yard.

For sure check out Rick Austin's gardening and greenhouse books in the Reference Section.

John Denver used to use herbs as cologne and he did all right with the ladies. Herbs will keep the flies off your back porch and momma can go right out the door and snatch up some seasoning for supper. Borage, Lavender, Bee Balm and spices triple as beautiful edible flowers and attract those all-important bees and wasps to your garden. Of course, I go foraging into my back woods for wild editable, berries and fruit and food as well. Roses and many kinds of flowers and weeds are edible and good for medicinal purposes, so spread them around your yard and, shuuuu! It's a secret. Check out the chapter below on wild edibles and the like.

PLANTING IN POTS

Anything can be planted in pots which makes it easier to isolate crops and easily moveable (using your neighbor's dolly). The size, type and decor is endless. They lend themselves nicely to pouch and deck gardens, and can be quite decorative too. It's kinda nice to step out on the deck of a condo in the city and nip some greens or herbs for dinner.

You can use potting soil or the same mix as your garden, only lean a bit toward the loosely packed soil, good drainage pots. And remember to water and feed the plants, same as your regular garden. Some rotted straw or perlite mixed in can help keep moisture regulated. Tomatoes (staked or caged), peppers, potatoes, Bush beans, herbs, ginger, onions, just about anything you want will grow nicely in pots. Tend and water like you would with your garden.

Next, I'm going to try some rotten soggy straw in the bottom ⅓ of a 5 gallon bucket, or pot, to see if I don't have to water other than rain up here on Dry Ridge.

Summing it up, there are as many gardens as there is imagination. Be creative. Be innovative. Think rooftops, along sidewalks, porches, hanging gardens, patio, deck, indoors, window boxes and window gardens, especially year round kitchen herbs. Mix and match. Supplement your main garden. Don't forget secret gardens, in and amongst your flowers. And some flowers are edible. A green house is not just for starting plants; it can be a year round producer. A garden is a garden no matter how small.

HYDROPONIC GARDENING

Hydroponics is a form of gardening without soil, instead growing plants in a mixture of nutrient, oxygenated water and a artificial light where needed. As such, it is ideal for apartments and city dwellings. Hydroponics can be concentrated in small tiered places and lends itself to year round gardening. Of course, seedlings and seed saving and harvesting and storage are quite the same as any other type of gardening. It is best suited for growing greens of all kinds, as well as tomatoes and peppers. There are several methods of hydroponic gardening: the wick system, water culture, ebb and flow. The idea is to flow the nutrient over the plant roots. Of course getting the proper nutrient is key. That basil or garlic you suspend in a glass in the kitchen window year round is a simple example of hydroponics.

I'm not and expert by any means on this form of gardening. It certainly has been around for a while. It's a bit futuristic for my taste, but then, you ask, "What does the future hold in store for us?" However, the Internet and Utube is loaded with ample examples, and information on setting up and maintaining hydroponic crops. I would suggest starting with The Spruce for starters: https://www.thespruce.com/beginners-guide-to-hydroponics-1939215

GROW YOUR OWN SEEDLINGS

Start in February. You'll need pots, potting soil, trays, bottom tray that holds water, seeds, grow light helps and a spray bottle of hydrogen peroxide and water (1:5). If you like, you can spritz the soil before planting to keep down damping off. Get an inexpensive grow light to help with extending winter indoor growing to 16 hours. Plant in a bunch, then when they get their second leafs, break apart/thin out while soils is very wet so they untangle easy and plant in individual pots or direct into ground. With tomatoes, transplant seedlings. Lay the tomato seedling across a 4" pot with loose potting soil mix, poke a hole in the middle with the erasure end, then lay the seedling across the pot and with the edge of the pencil, ease the plant down into the soil so the roots don't show and just the leafs show. Next step is to set them out after last spring frost, deep into a dibber hole with the leafy part showing. Tomatoes love making a big healthy root clump.

Also try this unique way of starting seeds - "27 Gardening Hacks You'll Want to Know" https://youtu.be/jD8n2CKEWtA This is a very nicely done video of how to start and propagate plants in simple unique easy ways.

Hotbeds

A greenhouse or hotbed is a good place to grow food or harden off your new seedlings. A hot bed can be built temporarily right into as much of your raised bed as needed, using a PVC hoop design and clear plastic covering. Half inch PVC fits nicely into a six inch piece of 1" PVC, driven into the soil. You can also fashion the same hoop type hotbed attached to a 2x4 frame and hinged on one side and propped up with a board to hold it open as needed. Use zip ties to hold the plastic in place. You can regulate the temperature and humidity by raising or lowering the hot bed or by propping the ends open.

Greenhouses

There are many, many various greenhouse designs online. They vary from wooden or cattle panel frames covered with clear plastic all the way to glass houses attached to your house to free-standing glass greenhouses with built in ventilation.

WHEN WHAT HOW TO
PLANT BY TYPE OF PLANT

When to plant? Don't listen to me but best advice is wait till after the last frost. Trust Mother Nature. Your plants and seeds do. Notice how your perennials pop up at just the right time? Don't tell me plants aren't smart! Plants generally grow when the conditions are right, and so **why rush them** (with a few exceptions like carrots, garlic and radish). Definitely don't rush sweet potatoes, okra, cucumbers, squash. Pick up one of those handy "Planting Guides" from SowTru Seeds. They are a gardener-friendly national firm, located in Asheville. Check out their website.

Raised no weed garden bed and Hootie

On the other hand, I like to push the season a bit and cover my crops with straw if the temperature drops into the freeze/frost zone. However, some crops are cold hardy like carrots and garlic and spinach and can be planted in the fall or early Spring to pick late and winter over. Potatoes tolerate early planting (but frost can nip them), as do onions and lettuce.

1. Tomatoes: plant 4 to a 7 foot 2x2 stake, with the poles spaced about two feet apart. Fertilizer with epsom salt and treat plants (& roses) for black spot: 2 aspirin+2 tbl baking soda/gal. Blossom End Rot or Yellow leaves with green veins: 2/700mg Tums/gal. water/sprayer. Sucker plants by pinching off any new shoots out from stalk. You can leave one natural

35

sucker. You'll recognize it toward the bottom as stalk grows upward. I recommend heirloom tomatoes because you can save the seeds and they are proven brands: Cherokee, Abe Lincoln, Mortgage Lifter, Arkansas Traveler, Rose, Titan, Mennonite. Good hybrids are: Better Boy, Big Boy, Beefsteak, Rutgers.

2. Peppers - prune plant top at start to create bushy plant. Fertilizer and spray same as tomatoes. Pick your peppers, tomatoes, beans, okra, squash, cucumbers regularly; otherwise the plant will figure it done good and will quit producing!

3. Potatoes - I plant red, yellow and russets in my Ruth Stout no-dig, no-water garden plot. I plant about 40 plants in a 20x20 foot plot. I plant them in April cause they like the cool weather. Mound old straw mulch (or dirt) up on potato stalks as they grow for bigger yield. I also have four potato towers made of 5' hog wire in a 3' diameter cylindrical shape, anchored to a t-pole. I've cut access holes to reach in to get the potatoes but wear gloves and a long sleeve sweatshirt to keep from getting wire pricks! Store potatoes in cool dry dark place.

4. Lettuce - plant early spring and second crop in September.

5. Cabbage - plant about two feet apart and look out for those pesky little white butterflies that lay cabbage worms on the back of leaves. Squish them daily and use natural neem oil to protect the plant. They do sell a mess cloth to cover the cabbage family. Keep yellowed leafs trimmed out. The whole plant leafs and all is edible. Red cabbage can enhance your secret gardens around the yard.

6. Sweet Potatoes - plant from shoots after the last frost in loose soil. Some runners will take root but just allow a few. Keep the vines trimmed a bit so the nutrient will go to the tubers. Sweet potato vines make an attractive grown cover in your secret flower bed gardens too. Then voila in the fall - surprise! - big healthy bonus Beauregard potatoes.

7. Cucumbers - Trellis using a cattle panel arch (or a smaller trellis arch made of hog fence). Grow pickle size and slicing kind. Pick before they get too big. Keep mulched for constant moisture. Watch out for stink bugs, lady bug like orangish leaf eating beetles and powdery mildew on leafs (trim those leafs off and compost).

8. Pole Beans, Lima's and Peas - You can plant bush beans, but they take up a lot of room. Plant bush beans around places in yard in and

amongst your flowers. I prefer to trellis Pole Beans on light green 4"
by 5' netting by 60" nylon trellis netting you get at Tractor Supply or
on Amazon. I toss it over a 2x2x8 fixed to the top of two end 2x2x8
poles screwed into the raised box, about six inches from the side of the
raised garden box. I anchor the trellis netting on one side to roofing
nails, driven halfway in (so's to hook the trellis netting to) spaced 2"
apart on the outside of the raised bed frame, then anchor netting to a
2x2x8 running lengthwise screwed down on the raised bed frame 20"
out from the side of the raised bed with roofing nails in it too. (check
out the photo). Essentially the netting forms a steep tent-like trellis to
accommodate two rows of 40 been plants each in an eight foot long
garden box. That will give you a bushel of good ole' Golden Romano
from that one two-sided trellis. Before planting your beans inoculate
them with a nitrogen fixing solution and punch holes about an inch
deep with your index and little finger. Drop in a bean into each hole,
cover with soil and pat the earth gently to snug the bean into the soil
for good germination. Top dress with epsom salt and perhaps some
cured chicken manure. They'll pop up and find the trellis and climb
as high as high as eight feet. Beans like water and food regularly. Beans
are a legume, meaning they fix nitrogen in the soil. You are gonna have
to pick your beans every day, so's the plant thinks it has to produce
more beans. Otherwise the plants will stop putting out new beans. I
spray my beans with my aspirin/baking soda solution. CAUTION:
Catch bean beetles early and treat immediately and regularly (with
diatomaceous earth spray solution as needed) to avoid an infestation.
Wasps and birds will help keep the bugs off your beans and plants.
In an infestation, you'll wanna blast the beetle worms with grandpa's
12 gauge, but that tends to blow holes in the beans! Use a beetle trap
instead.

9. Carrots - plant early spring and fall (to winter over). In very loose soil
    mix in perlite, bone meal (phosphorus), epsom salt, potting mix on
    top. Use seed strips or punch holes 2" apart using first two fingers or
    a dibber. Cover with a light layer of soil, sprinkle, spread newspaper
    over bed and keep wet a couple weeks till carrots germinate then thin
    by harvesting young carrots. And alternate method is to make shallow
    furrows and sprinkle seeds in by hand, then lightly cover and gently

tamp soil down and keep wet till carrots pop up.

10. Okra - I prefer red okra, a medium sized prolific okra. Start from seeds or plant directly into the garden. Pick them daily, along with asparagus, beans and tomatoes. You can't rush okra. It likes warm nights.

11. Onions - plant in fall and plant around fruit tree perimeter and other places throughout your garden to ward off pests. For big

softball onions, plant from seeds six weeks before the first or last frost. Plant 2" apart and harvest every other one for green table onions. Best yellow varieties are Texas Legends and Walla Walla. Sweet White is good and reds, while not as large are very good to grow. Top prune. your onions to encourage bigger onions, then use tops to flavor foods. If you use onion starts they make green onions best. Plant the roots only to get a larger onion. They will seem like they're going to fall over but they won't and they will make a very large onion. But **it's best to plant from seed if you want the biggest onions**.

12. Garlic - plant in fall to winter over. Side dress with high nitrogen (I use dry cured chicken manure) at first to grow nice and tall healthy green stems. The heartier and bigger the tops, the bigger and more cloves you'll get. But prune a few inches off the top to encourage more stems. Note that seed stem that suddenly appears is a delicacy - pick them and eat them asap. Harvest fresh when needed. Harvest the crop when the the first third of the outer leaves die back. Hang garlic with its papery cover, braided up to dry on screen porch. In three weeks when it's thoroughly dry (cut a stem down by the bulb to check), store. Onions, garlic, spinach and hearty greens and kale will winter over in moderate zones. Treat leeks same as garlic but eat them fresh. Leek with cream cheese is a tradition at the Indy 500.

13. Roses: prune back die-back and remove debris and use aspirin/soda spray and epsom salt. If you live in the North Country, trim roses back,

mulch and cover with a styrofoam rose cover. Remove debris from around the base.

14. Berry Bushes: Trim dead stuff offa your blueberry bushes and grapes (and roses) in the spring. I use that black half inch orchard netting stretched over pvc ½ inch hoops and anchored to the ground with landscape staples, to cover my blueberries. Cut vertical slits, that the birds can't see, to reach your hand in for a great in garden treat. NOTE: The birds will strip you blueberry bushes the exact day they ripen - thus the orchard netting. Bears can smell over-ripe blueberries a mile away; so plan your harvest and you won't have any bear problems. And remember, if Mr. Bear gets into your stuff; it's his stuff today! Don't argue with a bear.

15. Grapes: Trellis on wire stretched between t-fence poles. In fall trim back your grapes to leave only a couple of buds where this years growth meets last years old vine. Do that every year. In spring leave only 2 runners per wire to grow this year's grapes. You'll get bigger, healthier, clusters using this vineyard method of pruning.

And don't forget to start picking and eating ASAP throughout the entire season. You do no have to wait. Enjoy early pickings! Me and Joe used to ride the old mule sled between corn rows stripping off those fresh ears (two per stalk) into the sled and eating a fresh raw occasional ear or two along the way - Ummm tasty! Peas are just too darn sweet picked right outta the garden. Tomatoes are a given for eating right off the vine. And rob a few new potatoes and yams early. My wife has no idea how prolific my blueberries are.

Plant direct into the soil

"*Dibber*"

When you plant directly in the soil whether seeds or transplanted seedlings, be sure to water them good right after planting.

1. Tomatoes: Don't be afraid to purchase plants from Lowes and such. The Better Boy hybrids are big producers. Pinch off all lower limbs and plant deep using your dibber. Make a hole wide enough for the plant ball and push deep ¾ ways down into garden soil. Nothing fancy. Just a hole, pinch off lower limbs, push plant snug into hole, backfill and DONE. I have found "Bonnie's Grape (TAMI-G)" to be an extremely prolific pole indeterminate, hybrid grape tomato. It was a wonderfully rich tomato taste, thin skin and produces to the frost. I get about 300 tomatoes off each plant. Give the Cherokee Purple brand a try too. Don't plant tomatoes too soon!

2. Potatoes: cut seed potatoes the day before leaving two eyes per. You can dig a trough and place in dirt eyes up, than mound dirt up as plant grows. Or just stick down into the rotten hay and walk away! No digging, no watering required with Ruth Stout Method. Potatoes are frost sensitive.

3. Onions: Plant roots only if you want big onions. Otherwise, poke a hole with finger and stick shoot into it. DONE.

4. Asparagus and rhubarb: Purchase crowns from store and expect fruit the second year. Separate crowns as plants mature to get some "free plants." Leave one shoot per asparagus plant toward end of season to feed the root system.

5. Carrots: Require really, really, really soft loose soil. Don't worry about thinning out carrots. Just pick the small ones and eat 'em! Use your dibber or trowel or a gloved hand to make a very shallow ditch to sprinkle the seeds in, back fill with the dirt and pat firmly. Radishes are the same. Both do well in the shade between two rows of tomatoes.

6. Plant all rest of garden seeds direct into dirt. Poke a hole with your finger and drop in a bean every 4". Generally an inch deep for big

seeds, a half inch for small seeds. Cover and gently pat down the soil and water or you can plant in a fresh Spring rain.

7. I have found seed tapes great when you get my age and those tiny seeds get smaller and smaller.

8. Check out James Prigioni's video on how to get the most crops out of your raised bed garden. It is a bit overkill, as he divides a 10X4 foot raised bed into 40 one foot squares. But also pay close attention to how he spaces and plants carrots and beets. I think this would be a great way if you only have one raised bed. https://youtu.be/OXbhQOqvcwk

NOTE: Be sure to harvest and replant basil every week. I have had great success with drying or dehydrating basil, dill, chives, garlic, ginger etc on low heat to crush up and put in decorative jelly jars. After dry, pulverize in a coffee mill.

Beauties from my friend Ed Foster, May He Rest In Peace

HARVESTING AND STORAGE

1. **Tomatoes** - pick them daily. Trim the plants up as you pick. Birds, wasps and stink bugs love em too, so if they are beginning to ripe you can go ahead and pick them. They will finish ripening inside and still taste like home grown maters. Eat them right off the vine. Eat em fresh, perhaps with a dash of salt and pepper. They freeze well too. Just quarter them, flash freeze on a tray and vacuum seal for best results. Ummm, I love a mater samwich with mayonnaise on sunbeam bread "Just like my infield," Bobby Self would say, "No holes in in it!" Bobby coached my daughter and the "Bandits" girls softball team to ninth in the nation in Vidalia, Georgia, but's that's a story in itself.

2. **Potatoes** - harvest some all summer. Fresh smaller potatoes are just simply delicious. Later, when the tops begin to whither, after some plants have flowered, fork them out of the ground and brush them off and lay them out to cure for a week. Then separate into sizes and eat the smaller ones first and any cut or damaged ones. The larger ones will keep in your cool, dark root cellar till Spring. Plant what you have left. NOTE: If you used the Ruth Stout method of planting in thick rotted straw, all you have to do is spread the straw and find those golden beauties. No digging and they are clean as a whistle.

3. **Sweet Potatoes** - plant after frost, keep vines trimmed and harvest well into October before the freeze. Sweet potatoes need to be cured for a week or two to set their sugar. Sweet potatoes have a rich showy vine. I plant them in my flower gardens and nobody is the wiser till Fall. They also do well in a Ruth Stout Garden.

4. **Beans** - Pick your beans daily. That way the plant will think it needs to keep growing beans and you'll get a bigger, longer harvest. I absolutely love Golden Gate Romano pole beans. They are a prolific crop. The beans get sometimes a foot long and are uh-um tender and stringless. Save some back and dry them for next year's seeds. You can can 'em even freeze 'em, that is if you don't gobble them up first.

5. **Bell Peppers** - Harvest as you wish, any size. They freeze well. I cut them in half and take the seeds out (save some for planting). Yum, I love stuffed bell peppers!

6. **Lettuce** and other leafy plants - pick/prune leaf-by-leaf daily. Lettuce is a hardy crop. Keep planting it all season.

7. **Carrots and Radish** and other underground veggies - pick them all season as you thin them out and yes they will stork in a cool dark place.

8. **Onions** - Plant them finger deep for fresh green onions. Plant just the roots for big onions to slice and spice and store. Store just like your potatoes. Plant in Fall and Spring. Eat them all season.

9. **Garlic** - Plant in fall. Harvest when the tops wilt back. Keep the tops trimmed to encourage more and bigger cloves. Eat fresh garlic all season. Braid and hang up on the screen porch to dry. Save a few cloves for replanting in the Fall.

10. **Okra** - My favorite (Chris' okra book at SowTru Seeds) is Red Okra. Okra is a long-to-harvest food, but worth it. Clip off the okra daily. The plants get tall, so plant them accordingly. When I was young, we used to eat slimy-cooked okra and line the ends up around your plate.

11. **Asparagus** - Harvest these little secret growers. In the Spring they shoot up quick. You may need to eat the right out of the garden. Pick regular, daily, so they don't go to seed. Let the last few stalks in late summer develop and go to seed so they feed the tubers for next year. Remember, voles love the tubers, so keep an eye out or plant a little catnip in your garden to attract the neighbor's cat to keep your garden rodent free.

12. **Cabbage** Family Plants - plant early and late. They love the cold. And look out for the tiny cute white butterflies, cause they're laying worm eggs on your cabbages! Aphids love broccoli. Hey wait! You can eat the leafs too!

13. **Zucchini and Squash** - Pick daily and trim the lower wilted leaves back regularly to keep down the mildew, looking for those pesky squash bugs. Just squish 'em and the yellow eggs underneath the leaves. Winter squashes come in later and save nicely. Trellis zucchini.

14. **Sunflowers** - When the heads droop, clip off with about 2' of stalk and rub off the spent buds covering the seeds, tie up in threes with twine and hang upside down in your shed or barn or screen pouch. The seeds are mature but need to be air dried. Harvest seeds. Save a few to plant next year. I have had some Russian Mammoth Sunflowers with the head 18" across.

15. **Herbs** - Plant and replant all season and grow indoors too. Most are perennials if the freeze doesn't grab 'em. Prune basil just above a stem juncture to promote bushing out. Don't let it flower! Try this with your herbs: strip leaves off the stem fresh and chop up, add a dash of olive oil and freeze in muffin pans. Then store the frozen bricks in airtight ziplock.

Storage

You have planted. Early crops, second crops, winter-over crops and perennials. You've enjoyed good fresh vegetables all summer and into the fall. Now let's find out how to store your veggies so as to make it to the spring harvest. You can store root crops like potatoes and onions, garlic and winter squash in that cool dark place. Grandma had a root cellar for just that and more. You can can just about anything in quart or any size jars. You can even mix beans and taters in the same jar to make a testy meal in itself. Mark and date everything. That's a darned proven way to stretch your eats over a couple seasons. You can blanch and freeze and dehydrate fruits and vegetables. Just make sure you got electricity or a solar backup. I like to try to keep a full supply of all kinds of fruits and dehydrated vegetables and spices in Mason Jars with the lids on and a silicone dry pack in each, like those that come in your new shoe boxes and the like. Caution! Grandkids eat peaches and tomatoes and berries like candy!

YOUR SECOND GARDEN: 2ND PLANTINGS AND WINTER-OVER CROPS

You have planted Your spring garden and reaped the benefits. Now it's time to plant your second garden of the year and double your garden productivity. Don't be satisfied with just one growing season. After all you have good soil, you've composted and fertilized your garden. Don't waste it. Plant a second garden about mid-August. There are veggies that will do fine in fall and flourish, many beyond a frost, some crops will winter over such as garlic, onions, carrots, spinach, kale and all of your perennials. It's time to put in your second crop. Be sure to get your seeds early as most stores don't recognize second garden season.

Second Plantings I select from for July/August:
Beans, peas, potatoes, spinach, chard, kale, cabbage, arugula, radishes, garlic, leeks, onions, carrots, cucumbers, zucchini, beets, turnips, kohlrabi, herbs (chives, dill, basil, rosemary, oregano, sage, mints), lettuces, radishes, parsnips,

Plants That Winter Over:

1. Perennials: rhubarb, asparagus, dill, arugula, greens
2. Garlic, onions and leeks
3. Carrots
4. Spinach, collard, turnip and all sorts of greens, you can even extend your lettuce and salad greens or new seeds if you cover them right in the garden with a big translucent storage bins like you get at Loews. A greenhouse comes in handy.
5. Herbs: mints, rosemary, oregano, sage, thyme, ginger,

6. Bring your lemon trees into shelter in cold climates.
7. It's also time to propagate apple seeds and air rooting apple and blueberry bushes

Perennials

Set aside sections of your gardens for perennials and mark them "Do Not Disturb" or "See You Next Spring!"

1. Rhubarb (split crown)
2. Asparagus (split crown)
3. Garlic (replant part of harvest in fall)
4. Potatoes (leave a few in the Ruth Stout Garden at harvest)
5. Jerusalem Artichokes (split tubers and replant)
6. Ginger (split and replant in fall). Buy it in grocery store.
7. Berries (Blue, Black, Raspberry, Currants, June Berries (cuttings and seeds)
8. Grapes (cuttings)
9. Apples (cuttings and seeds)
10. Let some plants go to seed (spinach, leeks, onions, turnips, radishes, lettuce
11. Save seeds, clean and store in cool dry dark place (beans, tomatoes, dill, squash, zucchini, cucumbers, carrots, turnips, beets, lettuce and of course edible flowers like Borage.

Don't forget to let your perennials reseed themselves and feed their roots. Late in the season leave one stalk from each asparagus to grow bushy from each asparagus to replenish the rhizomes.

You Hungry?

You can grow some things very, very fast. And some things you can grow all year long. And then, don't forget the, Rick Austin Indoor Garden. And thank God for perennials.

Think about starting these fast growing veggies: radishes, carrots, loose leaf lettuce, all types of greens (chop, Swiss chard, collard greens, spinach, turnip greens), spring onions and peas. In fact you can start in early on the foliage of peas. As you can eat the foliage of turnips, turnip greens. https://youtu.be/CgG7XLK4RA0

And that's why you planted those fall winter-hardy crops, to grow and harvest and eat all winter, like carrots, spinach, collards, onions, leeks and garlic. Rosemary bushes and some hardy herbs winter over the further south you get. But, hey, just plant them inside and set 'em in the kitchen window. That-a'ways, their handy and they are fragrant and attractive plants.

The more you grow inside the more you have to eat all year long. Be sure to check out the nifty ideas and detailed add-on hot-house plans of Rick Austin in the references. Rick has a whole series of homestead prepper books.

Learn how to prepare delicious meals from your garden and from your stored harvest.

Munch-a-Lunch

One of the joys of home gardening is that you can eat fresh stuff right there, right in the garden. I call it munch-a-lunch. With or without sweet tea with mint, dill or herbs, or a cold sweaty long neck, just stroll along and gather up some carrots, radish, turnip, beet, lettuce, green onions or fresh pruned garlic tops and other greens and their bulbs and roots, then snatch a fresh asparagus and you have a gourmet lunch. Toss in a tomato or eat it like an apple with juice running off your chin and voila! Instant munch-a-lunch. The menu grows with the season. And beets and turnips, parsnips and such. Desert? Well there's those strawberries and blueberries that the birds haven't seen yet. Yummy. Enjoy!

How to Propagate (free plants)

Think about trying your hand at propagating plants, vegetables, roses, fruit trees and the like. I learned to take a healthy cutting off a woody plant and slice the stem at an angle, rough up the bottom ares, dip it in some root-tone power and poke it in the ground or pot and keep it moist and humid. Transplant it when it develops roots.

That worked for my dad but I haven't had much luck. I think primarily because it needs to be tended to too often. I have found very helpful information on Utube.

Here is a must see Utube video you will want to watch for starting and propagating all kinds of fruits and vegetables. It is nicely done showing simple, easy, unique ways to start and propagate seeds. You need to watch it and take notes and reference it. Propagating can be difficult or fun. I prefer the latter. https://youtu.be/jD8n2CKEWtA

SAVING SEEDS

To save seeds, harvest heritage type only, clean, dry and store in cool, dark, place in marked containers for next year. Essentially, you need to gather seeds for at least one of each heritage plants. Harvest beans when they are dry. Tomatoes, cucumbers, squashes, zucchini, cantaloupe, etc. all need to be fermented (to get the anti-sprouting gel coat off) in small glass in their own juice (or add a small bit of water) a couple days (good seeds will fall to the bottom) then use strainer to washed, then air dried on a paper plate, then put in airtight containers or ziplock bags with a small rolled up dry paper towel piece to absorb any moisture. Mark type and date and store in a cool, dry, dark place, like a closet, protected from pests. Don't forget to save flower seeds too.

You can't save seeds from hybrid tomatoes or corn. Be concerned that plants of different varieties can cross pollinate and give you seeds of whatever. You yourself may want to look up how to self-pollinate certain vegetables to assure quality of the seeds.

You can grow lemon and other citrus and fruit trees from seed or cuttings. Get a lemon you like and cut in two and dig out seeds with your fingers. Holding them individually with a paper towel (because they are tiny little slippery devils) and with your fingernails peel off the outer layer. Place several seeds on a paper towel and fold in too twice, moist em and place in a ziplock and date and mark bag. Place in cool dark place. They will begin to sprout in two weeks. Once there is a healthy tap root, plant in a container. Lemon trees: like sunny spot, mulch to their drip line, commercial citrus plus fertilizer, plenty of water. Prune off disease limbs. Don't worry about pests if you have followed my planting guide. The trees are resilient and strong and can fight off disease. Watch for the tale-tale sawdust around bore holes and take action and prune. Do the same for apple seeds, etc.

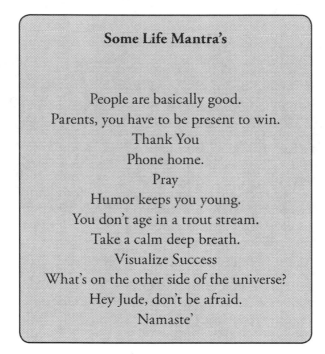

Some Life Mantra's

People are basically good.
Parents, you have to be present to win.
Thank You
Phone home.
Pray
Humor keeps you young.
You don't age in a trout stream.
Take a calm deep breath.
Visualize Success
What's on the other side of the universe?
Hey Jude, don't be afraid.
Namaste'

HOW TO MAKE SEED TAPES

1. Best for small seeds like carrots, radishes, beets, turnips, spinach, lettuce, etc., seeds you sow directly into the garden, but want to space out. Now, mind you, I will sprinkle a plot with carrot seeds by hand and not bother thinning them out. That-a-way they shade the weeds out and if

Making seed tapes in the winter

your soil is soft rich loose sandy loam (the kind where you can easily stick your whole hand down past your wrist) and perlite, the carrots will do just fine and you'll have plenty of varying size carrots. But you may want to try seed-tapes.

2. Cut desired length paper towels into 1" strips, glided together for longer tapes.

3. Put dots using marker pen at 2" to 4" apart to indicate where seed will be placed (work on an old table or cardboard, so as to not soil momma's dinner table.

4. Mix up thoroughly a thin paste of heaping tablespoon of flour and water in a small bowl or cup.

5. Open seed packet and spread seeds out on a white paper plate so they are easy to pick up.

6. Using a chop stick, shish kebab stick or eraser end of a pencil, place a drop of paste on a dot on the paper strip, then use the stick to pick up a seed and place into the glue dot.

7.   Mark the seed strip for type of seed and let dry completely.
8.   Wad up the dried strips and place into a marked zip lock bag for use when planting.

The seed tape technique saves on seeds and assures proper spacing in garden rows. It can be prepared in winter and don't forget to get the grandchildren involved in making seed strips and planting them! I haven't had much luck with carrots. I prefer to hand plant and thin by harvesting those tender young carrots.

Another very interesting way of starting plants like carrots, peppers, cucumbers and squash and the like can be found at "27 Gardening Hacks You'll Want to Know" https://youtu.be/jD8n2CKEWtA This is a very nicely done video of how to start and propagate plants in simple unique easy ways. it looks like fun to me. It suggests ways to prepare seeds by soaking, rolling up in a paper towel at 3" spacing, then unrolling in a planting trench or row and covering lightly with dirt. Let me know if it works for you.

HOW TO TAKE CARE OF PLANTS: PESTS AND NATURAL POTIONS

First off, get a bird feeder and birdbath. The bees and ladybugs need a drink too. Spray your birdseed with cayenne pepper to ward off squirrels and bears.

Don't plant where the sun don't shine! Plants get their energy from the sun. Gardening is location, location, location! Natural gardening works mighty fine. Good soil, mulch and proper watering is the key. Put a seed in the ground and it will grow. And pick off and squish them pests and shoo the crows away. I try to stay away from chemical pesticides and fertilizers. There are many natural ways to tend to your garden. I am not an organic gardener by intent, it just turns out that way. I am lucky to have two beekeepers within a half mile as the crow flies, and a plethora of bumble bees from God knows where!

Here's a good rule of green thumb - plant your aromatic herbs and mints, onions, leeks and garlic at the corners of your garden and around your berry bushes and fruit trees. Marigolds are a must, beautiful and drive away pests for years to come from one planting (Save the seeds). They'll keep the flys, gnats and mosquitos away as well. Vinegar soaked rags laying around are good. Irish Spring soap cubes on the corners of your garden boxes will keep bugs, pests, rabbits, rodents and deer out of the garden. If you started from a lawn, treat the entire area with milky spore mix. I like the 20 pound sacks of granular milky spore from Amazon. The stuff lasts in the soil for five or six years. And remember, no grubs, no Japanese beetles, no voles! Problem solved naturally.

Another good pest control is a dog and a cat. I don't always have either around but my neighbor has a good watch dog, to scare off the rabbits, raccoons, ground hogs and bears. I plant catnip in and around my garden. The kitties keep the varmint population down. And, again, put out a bowl of water and have bird baths to keep my gardening birds, lady bugs and buddies happy.

Here are some helpful tips on plant care:

1. MILKY SPORE GRANULES: (every 4 years) - for Japanese Beatles and grubs and such. A teaspoon every four feet in your garden and surrounding area. It is a natural bacteria and won't harm worms and good insects. It's organic. No grubs; no moles. One treatment lasts four years. Four tbls dish soap with water and spray on the beetles.
2. CALCIUM: (2 wks) 2 Tums/gal for tomatoes, peppers. Spray ground around the plants. Also use eggshells.
3. NEEM Oil: Get the real stuff. It doesn't take much (iron phosphate). 1 tsp/16 oz or 2 tbl/gal plus 10 drops soap (as oil and water don't stay mixed) and shake frequently as you apply with a sprayer. Spray greens thoroughly front and back of leafs and help by squashing those orangish egg clusters on the back of leafs. Spray weekly or daily during an infestation of those pesky cute little white butterflies. AND spray with a good soapy mixture and get some Japanese Beetle traps and place 30' from your garden.
4. ASPRIN, BAKING SODA, NEEM OIL, SOAP. ALL PURPOSE SOLUTION: water (gal) + 2 crushed aspirin + 2 crushed Tums, baking soda (2 tbl)+ (4 tsp) neem oil (or vegetable or olive oil) + 10 drops of soap and shake well frequently - For tomatoes, peppers and roses, any and all plants as needed.

> **ALL PURPOSE CONCOCTION: water (gal) + 2 crushed aspirin + 2 crushed Tums, baking soda (2 tbl)+ 2 tsp neem oil + 10 drops of soap and shake well frequently. Keep handy in a garden sprayer.**

5. VINEGAR; Will deter all varmints and pests from the garden. Leave a couple of small ventilated jars (or rags) throughout the garden with a ½ cup of 100% white vinegar. DO NOT SPRAY PLANTS WITH

VINEGAR. I heard a tablespoon of mothered apple cider vinegar every night is good for what ails you too. Same for a tablespoon of real honey every day (and scratch yourself in the garden, cause you weren't using long sleeves and gloves, put some honey on it.) Real honey is a natural wound anti-bacterial, healing medicine. So is pine tar.

6. IRISH SPRING SOAP: Place a 1" cube of that nasty smelling green Irish Spring soap chunks at each corner of your garden. It will deter rabbits, squirrels, skunks, possums, cats, even deer and rodents, moles and voles (although a ½ unchewed stick of Juicy Fruit gum into the mole hole will get rid of them pronto).

7. DUST: (at night as needed for chewing bugs & beatles) all plants with diatomaceous earth dust. Mix thoroughly (2 cups and 3 pumps of hand soap to gal, with water) and spray on. It effects the crawling chewing bugs, not the bees. It will harm ladybugs so be prudent.

8. Hedge your bet on a "bad year" or pest infestation - start more plants than you'll need. That-a-ways you'll be ready to replant should Mother Nature throw you a surprise.

9. HOW TO GET RID OF ANTS. There are many ways to get rid of ants. You can flood them, pour boiling water on the colony or put another colony on top of the first colony, creating an "ant war!" I personally prefer this organic method. First locate the ant hill or colony. Then mix up a pint paste of 1 part borax power to 1 part sugar. Place it directly on top of the roughed up ant hill. Voila ants disappear.

10. SLUGS - Lots of ways to rid slugs to getting them drunk! Yep, jar caps filled with beer placed strategically around in the garden works fine. Then sit back with a couple beers in the evening - one for you and one for the slugs.

11. FERTILIZER: (monthly) garden, trees, grapes, blueberries. Use cured cow or chicken manure, compost, rotting straw and grass clippings.

12. EPSOM SALTS: It is a great fertilizer. Weekly sprinkle around plants as fertilizer

13. TRIM (sucker as needed) Tomatoes (indeterminate Plants, the ones that put out a single stalk), peppers, cukes, squash, zucchini, cabbage, etc.

14. **SPANK**: (daily) tomatoes. Twiddle the blossoms daily with your first and second finger or at least shake the plants or whatever they are staked to. This will assure better pollination and a fuller crop. Tomatoes self pollinate.

15. INOCULATE: (beans before planting). Beans are a natural legume and help fix nitrogen into the soil.
16. WASH PLANTS: (2days) to rid white fly eggs on back of cabbage. If you plant cabbage, those pesky tiny white butterflies will come. Be vigilant.
17. ROSES need special care: Good soil, prune problems, prune at angle, clean clippers with alcohol or hydrogen peroxide after every clip, dispose of clippings and diseased pedals, put neem oil, SAAF, or turmeric power on cuts.
18. Got thrip? You gotta get aphids. Got aphids? Get the ladybugs to come around. They like a bush to winter over in and put out some water for them (and your neighbor's free-range mouser).
19. JUICY FRUIT GUM kills moles (and voles). Just drop ½ stick into opening. Chew the other half.
20. WATER: (regularly) Don't let the soil crust! I mention the gardens that don't need watering in the "Types of Gardens" section.
21. MULCH: Regularly for weed control and retain moisture and provide bacterial breakdown so plants and trees can absorb nutrients better. That white stuff you see underneath your rotting grass clippings is a natural bacteria that helps breakdown nutrients for plants and around fruit trees. Generally speaking if you can put your fist down into the soil, potatoes and carrots and the like will love it! If not, add more compost old straw or perlite. The underground crops thrive in loose soil.
22. **Intercropping**: Plant crops intermingled. Inside the tomato rows and bean trellis, plant shade loving plants like, basil, thyme, lettuce and radish. Outside the tall plants plant a strip of sun loving plants that won't interfere with sunlight or airflow or compete for nitrogen, like peppers, carrots, beets, parsnips, onions, garlic, leeks, rutabagas, and other phosphorus-loving root plants. Not spinach. Experiment a bit with which plants like each other? In nature's secret gardens, which plants grow together?
23. **Natural pesticides**: Plant onions, garlic, scented herbs and marigolds around the garden perimeter and fruit trees. Got thrip? Gotta get aphids! - Aphids eat thrip. Ladybugs lay larvae to eat aphids. So to attract Ladybugs, have bushes nearby and a pan of water. If you provide for them, they will come. And sure you may have a few holes in your rose and plant leafs but nature has a way of sharing and controlling things naturally. Oh and plant a little patch of catnip to attract the neighbor's

cat. Have a bird feeder nearby and spray birdseeds with cayenne pepper to keep the squirrels and bears out. I don't think birds have taste buds.

24. **Natural Repellants**: Vaseline ring around fruit trees and sunflower trunks to deter ants. Use Irish Spring soup cut up in small cubes at the corners of each bed. Nothing will cross that barrier. Nothing! No bears, voles, rabbits, mice, deer. No wonder I had so much trouble getting dates in high school! Replace as needed.

25. **Infestation**: All Purpose Pest Spray (above) -spray liberally or [Pyrethrum]

26. PLANT: See Sow True Chart (Replant in July/August and winter over garlic)

27. HARVEST: potatoes when foliage dies. After harvest set out regular potatoes to dry (don't wash). Then brush of any dirt with your glove and store in cool dark place. Sort out the small ones and damaged ones to use first. Cure sweet potatoes in cool dark for 2 wks to let the sugar set up in them.

28. STORAGE: Store all your onions and root crops in a cool dark dry place.

29. COLLECT SEEDS: throughout season select from best plant, clean the gel covering off, dry, mark & store in cool, dry, dark closet for the years to come.

30. Be Happy! Don't Worry!

Plant Care Schedule

You can casually plant your garden and walk away. And that's fine, especially if you've used Ruth Sloan's method of no digging, no weeding, no watering. But you won't! You won't because it's fun to tend a Garden, gets you out of the house into the sunshine.

A. **Prune** Peppers, onion and garlic tops, basil and Borage, zucchini (to prevent leaf mold and stem borers) and yellow squash. Sucker tomatoes and aggressively prune diseased leafs and other leaves out to increase airflow between plants. The object here is red not green. Don't let tomato leaves touch each other or touch the ground. Trim roses and sweet potato vines. You want tubers not green.

B. **Daily**! Pick beans, cucumbers and squash and asparagus. And pick off any tomato hornworms (ugg), beetles and squash bugs, caterpillars and feed to the chickens or put the on the bird feeder.

C. **Weekly** Plant Care: Add calcium (2 to 4 crushed up tums tablets/gallon of water and spray around the roots) especially for tomatoes; Use your ALL PURPOSE ORGANIC PEST SPRAY you made above: Spray any and all plants, rose black spot and fruit trees as needed for all kinds of pests, leaf dust and fungi; Feed worm beds kitchen scraps; Spray a diatomaceous earth and water solution on beans, tomatoes, roses, catch Japanese beetles, bean bugs and yellow larvae under leafs before they they hatch into an infestation!!! You know squashing bugs and pests is effective too - Ooey! Goey!

D. **Bi-monthly**: mulch with straw and grass clippings. Mulch around plants prevents weeds and creates that whitish bacteria that helps roots better absorb nutrition.

E. **Monthly**: Fertilize with Epsom Salt, natural chicken and cow fertilizer and compost. I compost my kitchen scraps in lock top worm buckets. Worms love garbage and so do bears. I caught one big black papa bear ripping a worm bed outta the ground and batting batting it around the yard! I just let him have at it watching out the window. He couldn't get it opened. Lesson learned for both of us.

Summary

Plant in sunny location, in good soil, straw and bales. Then attract worms and use natural fertilizers and compost regularly. Water as needed in morning. Spray all plants and roses with your special organic concoction in evening. Use Tums (calcium) spray around tomatoes to prevent end rot. Squish pests and use beetle traps. Sit in the shade and sip sweet tea and pray for good lady bugs, song birds and bees, health and world peace.

TYPICAL GARDEN PLANTS

I save seeds and buy seeds. I try to get the tried and true heritage types so's I can save the seeds from year to year. I start tomatoes from seed indoors starting in early March. The rest I plant direct into the ground, starting with cold crops and ending with beans and squash after last frost. I get some plants from Loews and TSC. Use the planting calendar guide from Sow Tru Seed and keep an eye on Mother Nature. The list below includes what I normally set out after the first or last frost. Check your particular area for the frost dates.

1. Tomatoes (30) Better Boy, Beefsteak, Abe Lincoln, Arkansas Traveler, Mortgage Lifter, Grape.
2. Beans (Romano2, KY Wonder Pole, King Lima Pole2, Green Arrow semi-pole Sweet Peas)
3. Potatoes (White, Yellow, Red)
4. Sweet Potatoes
5. Bell Peppers (Green, Red, Yellow)
6. Carrots (Tender, Danver, Nantes, Tenders)
7. Lettuce (Leaf, Romain)
8. Radishes (Try the while icicles)
9. All varieties of greens
10. Herbs of all kinds
11. Cabbages
12. Spinach
13. Turnips (shogun, Purple Tops)
14. Beets (Dark Red, Detroit)

*Roasted veggies straight
from the garden*

15. Onions (Red, Walla Walla, Texas Legend)
16. Leeks and chives
17. Okra
18. Tomatillos
19. Cucumbers (Marketmore, Boston, Muncher, pickling Bush)
20. Zucchini
21. Yellow Squash
22. Winter squash (Butternut and Spaghetti)
23. Rhubarb
24. Asparagus
25. Rutabaga
26. Corn (Early Golden Bantam)
27. Russian Mammoth Sunflower
28. Perennials will emerge on their own schedule
29. Arugula - perennial
30. Ginger - perennial
31. Shiitake Mushroom logs

NUTRITIONAL AND
DELICIOUS RECIPES

There are a jillion recipes, natural Rx and potions. These are but a sampling:

1. Hardtack - flour, teaspoon of salt and water. Need into dough. Roll out to ⅜" thickness. Cut into squares or use cookie cutter. Make holes like you find in Ritz Crackers all the way through. Bake in oven at 250 for 30 minutes a side. Done! Oh and don't even think of biting into them. They are called hardtack for a reason. Sometimes called "ship's biscuit because the store so well. Used as primary food for civil war troops, they are indestructible and store forever. Most soldiers and settlers would break off a piece in their mouth while they worked. Others would mix in soups, broths and joe. They are hard as a rock.
2. Ginger Tea - cinnamon and ginger.
3. Chi Tea from Trader Joe's
4. Chi Tea+ Mix in some ginger.
5. Cinnamon, ginger and honey tea.
6. Real Natural Honey - a tablespoon a day is good for what ails you. To test if honey is real, pot a glob in a small white cereal bowl and cover with tap water. Swirl it around and around for a minute and voila! A honeycomb pattern will appear. It's also good for cuts and abrasions.
7. Dehydrate: peaches, pineapple, apples.
8. Rose hip tea is refreshing on a cold winter's day.
9. Dandelions are edible and steep for a tea.
10. Apple Cider Vinegar drinks with a dash of ginger and lemon juice (8oz/day)
11. Muscle Cramps: potassium, magnesium, quinine, hydrate.

12. Daily Good for What Ails You: 8oz water, 1 teaspoon matcha power, ½ peeled lemon, ½ teaspoon grated ginger, ½ teaspoon ground cinnamon, honey - Blend.
13. Hot toddy and aroma therapy as needed.

Natural Rx (Do your homework before diving in here)

14. Wild Lettuce: dry leaves. pulverize, 1 tsp/cup hot water. Don't drink! Put on cuts and abrasions. Utube how to make a jar of potion. Use wisely as people have different tolerances to medicines.
15. Applesauce ginger - blend fresh ginger mix and mix with applesauce - 2 tsp/day Rx
16. Red Clover
17. Ginger Elixir: ⅓ ginger, ⅔ fresh sliced lemons and fill with honey to top. Use a tablespoon as Rx for colds and sore throat or just for fun. It helps with breathing.
18. Honey, garlic and ginger (1:1 covered with real honey). Let it sit over night. Refrigerate. It is a nice potion warmed. Tablespoon as needed
19. Honey can be used right on a wound.
20. Pine tar makes a great anti-bacterial bandage
21. Ginger
22. Cinnamon
23. Lemon
24. Honey
25. Cayenne Pepper
26. For healthy lungs: a cup of green tea in the morning, mixed with lemon juice, ginger, honey, cayenne pepper. See Motivational Doc reference.
27. Oregano is good for breathing problems
28. Turmeric
29. Although it is not natural, Tylenol (500) + ibuprofen (200) is considered to be the single best pain medication. Help stamp out opioid use.

Message from the Chestnut

As sure as Frost upon the virus lay,
The Tree will stand supreme again one day;
Though time may toll beyond our mortal means,
The Chestnut will again adorn the country scene.

For lo, these mortals will come to plant and spade,
And cultivate the chestnut day by day,
And return it will upon this hallowed ground,
For it once was dominant and renowned.

But just as weak as we all are too,
So does the Chestnut keep growing shoots anew;
And its persistence is supreme insight,
Lest we not persist and shrivel from a blight.

From *Poetry on My Mind* by Tom Tenbrunsel

THE AMERICAN CHESTNUT LEGEND

American Chestnut hybrid variety that is resistant to the blight

I was a member of the American Chestnut Foundation in its early years. I had witnessed the tree's resilience in "smoldering from the roots and sending up new shoots" according the Robert Frost. In his poem, Frost predicts the demise and recovery of the American Chestnut.

I've walked the Smokies with "Mr. American Chestnut," Herb Clabo, identifying the "old ghosts" of trees dead for decades, refusing to rot and fall over like most species. The US Forestry Service had to go into the Smokies National Park several decades back and fell the old ghosts, because their upright stance loaded with tannic acid made them explosive lightening rods.

I have seen the "Magnificent Seven" at Crystal Lake, Michigan - Seven (now six) healthy American Chestnut trees that escaped the blight. They are still used a a source of American Chestnut Seeds. I have even roasted a bag of them on an open fire (Prick them with a pocket knife first though or they will explode while roasting).

The American Chestnut (Castania dentata) once dominated the Appalachian range and was a major food source for animals, and tannic acid used in the tanning industry. Every railroad used chestnut ties before creosol ties because chestnut just never rots. Many a chestnut fence post is still standing on farms in these hills from the last century. The chestnut blight came from the import of oriental trees. The blight still persists on the eastern sea coast today.

Purchase and propagate the new hybrid and plant all over the place. I have two in my yard.

EDIBLE WEEDS

WILD EDIBLES

Free Food! Get familiar with your wild edibles. They are nutritious, delicious, especially in salads, and grow literally everywhere. Most are completely edible raw, in salads, smoothies or cooked. Get familiar with the ones that are edible and those that are not. Ease into eating wild edibles, don't mix to many until you know how your body reacts to them. There are good books and Utube videos (check out my references). Most have additional medicinal uses as well. The main ones to look for are: dandelions, chickweed, wild onions and garlic, henbit, wild clover, plantain, purslane, creeping charley, ground ivy, mustard weed (you'll know it because it smells mustardy), lams quarter, roses, daisies, miner's lettuce (find it in the shade), borage, wood sorrel (Indians chewed it on long trips to help with thirst), common mallow and most grasses. Remember as kids how we used to pull out the top part of grass and stick it in our mouth and chew on the tender lighter yellowish end? Well you do the same with cattails. That's the part you eat. Just break it off underwater and strip off the outer layer and eat the white clean pulp flesh. The Indians used the hotdog shaped top of cattails as flour.

Also get familiar with poisonous plants. Not all plants are edible. And certain parts of garden plants are not edible, like potato leafs, potato buds. They are in the deadly nightshade family. Cut off and green parts of a potato exposed to sunlight. See References for excellent Utube videos of edible, inedible and medicinal uses of plants. Also consult your doctor if you have a bad reaction to any food and using plants for medicinal purposes.

Naps Can Be Dangerous

"In my comfy chair where I sometimes rest between doing this and that and watching my garden grow, I sank into a cool breeze-induced, afternoon, shady nap, much as I often do these days.

Suddenly, half-awakened from a short sleepy-deep-nap sleep, I awoke! Startled! Immediately, I spotted the fright in the eyes of the old owl (in the photo) staring not at me but just behind me. Jezzz! I bolted upright from my chair, turned behind me, instinctively crouched in the ready position, gun drawn, only to feel like a fool! The friggin' owl's not real! I put it there myself, fool, to keep critters away. Wake up old man. Naps can be dangerous!"

From *Poetry on My Mind*, by Tom Tenbrunsel, iUniverse, 2020

BONUS CHAPTER: SURVIVAL ITEMS

1. A Plan - Be Prepared was my scout motto. Prepare for grid down and if it doesn't happen, well then take your stash down to the mission. Be realistic. Be discrete. Plan to work with your neighbors.

2. Food - A year's supply of staples and a garden (and heirloom seeds). Best way is to buy duplicates of what you have in your pantry (6 deep) when shopping. That's everything that is necessary and will keep and put in your pantry. Rotate. Prepare a weekly recipe. Items to stock up on: can goods of everything you like, including veggies, spam, tuna, salmon, herring, beans, rice, potatoes (store in cool dark place), potato power, milk power, peanut butter (it keeps), iodized salt, sugar, flour, yeast, baking soda and power, spices (barter items), spaghetti and sauces, real honey (test buy swirling a teaspoon in warm water in a white saucer. It's amazing. You'll recognize it immediately). Vacuum seal (get one that seals bags and mason jars for under $100) beans, flour, cereals and the like.

3. Water - 300 gallons and a source and filters. Have a rain barrel. Buy a large free standing Berkey filter ($450 but worth it). Pre-strain murky water in a clean dish towel or cheese cloth to extend the filter's life. Get a WaterBob and keep it in a bathroom cabinet. It is inexpensive and can be mighty handy in a emergency. It holds 100 gallons in a tub.

4. Shelter is Essential - your house plus lightweight tent/tarp, sleeping bags and complete ultralight camping equipment. (The Pocket Outdoor Survival Guide by J. Wayne Fears)

5. Fire - Know how to build a fire without matches or a lighter. Ferrocerium Rod & fat wood, consider a home wood stove for heat and cook on. Use iron pots to cook soup and chili in your wood stove or vented fireplace. Build an outdoor stove out of rocks or cinder blocks.

6. Candles, smokeless oil lamps, rechargeable flashlights with (18650 batteries are best).

7. Power for electricity/portable solar generator system (I use www.inergy. com)They are cheap and can run refrigerator, gas furnace and gas water heater, garage door, medical devices, lights (switch to LED), charge phones and laptops. Purchase a multi-fuel generator (it takes about 12000 watt generator to run a house) and run it on and off during the day, to save fuel. It takes about 8 gallons of gas or a tank of propane per day if you run it constantly.

8. Clothes, seasonal, shoes, rain poncho, toiletries, glasses, etc.

9. First Aid and Medical supplies & Rx, antibacterial ointment & OTC items

10. Support Group - Have a plan.

11. Tools, utensils & weapons

12. Transportation - bicycles/cars, extra gas/fuel, a good pair of boots and a furnished bug out bag

13. Cash, silver coins, liquor shots, spices to barter

What three crops would you grow for survival?

1. Well, the first crop is easy. What kept the Irish alive through sparse years under the thumb of England? Potatoes. Irish Potatoes. They are easy to grow, especially with the Ruth Stout no dig, no water garden and store well.

2. Beans. Beans are heavy producers, even with pests, they are nutritious, filling, and store well frozen, dry or canned. Get out your grandmother's gardening/canning notes.

3. Butternut squash. A no nonsense hardy, pest resistant, productive, flavorful, filling meal and they grow and store with no fuss.

4. Greens, spinach, collards, hardy greens, carrots, things that grow all year round are a distance fourth for me. Also remember to plan for a hothouse to grow all year long. See Rick Austin's reference. For preparedness, read One Second After by Bill Forstchen.

How much should I plant for my family to survive?

The question often arises, "How much should I plant for my family to survive?" Well, you can guesstimate, calculate, figure-ate, but it boils down to for how many and what they like to eat and where does your garden grow, Mary, Mary, quite contrary. Mainly, you want to grow and store enough to get you to the next growing season. There are many articles on this, but the best I've found is by Marie Iannoti in "The Spruce." She offers a simple estimate per number of plants, per square feet. Saving seeds is a part of surviving. There weren't many seed companies a few centuries back. Save and store and plant and tend your crops. I'd suggest to grow a bit extra (to share with neighbors).

How Much to Plant (For a Family of Four)

Asparagus	40 Plants	Perennial
Beets	10'	Spring and Fall Crop
Broccoli	5 Plants	Cool Season Crop
Brussels Sprouts	5 Plants	Cool Season Crop
Beans, Bush	15'	Succession Plant
Beans, Pole	3 Poles	Single Planting
Cabbage	5 Plants	Spring and Fall Crop
Carrots	10'	Succession Plant
Cauliflower	5 Plants	Spring and Fall Crop
Chard	5 Plants	Re-Grows after Harvesting Outer Leaves
Corn	15'	Succession Plant and Multiple Varieties
Cucumbers	2 hills	Single Planting
Greens	10'	Spring and Fall Crop
Kale	5 Plants	Single Planting
Lettuce, Leaf	10'	Succession Plant
Onions	5'	Single Planting
Peas	10'	Succession, Spring and Fall
Peppers	3 Plants	Single Planting
Radishes	5'	Succession Plant

by Marie Iannoti, thespruce.com

What happens when you cut through a Maple Tree log

BONUS CHAPTER ON
ULTRALIGHT CAMPING

Travel ultralight and carry things that have dual purpose.

Fire
- Baton knife
- Ferrocene fire stick
- Find fat wood along the way
- Shavings, feather stick, larger fat wood, sticks of increasing size then logs.

Water
- Carry only enough water in your container to get to the next water. Take breaks and camp by water.
- Filter: Use Aqua filter packed with 2 liter bladder in special cut-off water bottle with cap

Shelter:
- Ultralight single walled tent with plastic ground cloth
- Sleeping bag (plus silk or fleece liner), closed foam mattress (triples as a seat and back support in pack). Sleeping bag can be dangerous. Always provide an adequate breathing hole.

Clothing:
- Polypropylene (Capilene) base layer upper and lower as needed,
- Fleece stocking cap (35% heat escapes at night)
- Wear same clothes everyday, extra pair of socks (use as extra support in pack straps), with liners for long hikes. I prefer a trout fishing shirt with lots of pockets.

- I prefer lightweight low cut trail shoes (Altas) wet but dry easily for summer and waterproof ankle length boots for winter, all with aggressive treads.
- Dry clothes by wearing them or putting them on top of you in sleeping bag. They will dry easier. In below freezing, put your boots and water in your sleeping bag, or bury water in snow to keep from freezing.

Food:
- High Calorie Food You Like
- Breakfast bars, Lunch snacks, trail snacks, dinner freeze dried with extra rice and spices
- Utensils: spoon
- Eat edible berries

Miscellaneous
- Knife, folding saw, metal drinking and cooking cup (doubles as cook cup), first aid, floss (doubles as mending thread), toothbrush, small amount of duct tape wrapped around sharpie, safety pin (fish hook), a hiking stick gives you stability along precarious trails and crossings (also doubles as tent poles).
- Bring 50' paracord and three carabiners to tie your food up in tree at all times.
- Be smart. Use your hiking stick to check for snakes as you hop over logs and rocks. Don't surprise animals with cubs, if a screech owl happens into camp at midnight, try not to crap your sleeping bag!
- People are generally good. Hiking with friend(s) is preferred. I am enjoying teaching my pack mule grandkids hiking and nature. Carry is your preference (especially women).
- Ultralight pack

REFERENCES

1. Victory Gardens of WWII
2. Sow True Seed Company, Asheville, NC - seeds, starts, planting guide, sage advice. https://sowtrueseed.com/
3. Michigan Gardener is a favorite. I would just "subscribe" to his Utube page if I were you. You can get seeds from him too https://www.youtube.com/user/MIgardener Migardner has a great video on why you don't need to rotate your crops in a small garden https://youtu.be/ki2Xc8s44sI You can Utube all sorts of stuff.
4. Huws Richards Organic Gardening https://www.youtube.com/user/HuwsNursery
5. Gardening Channel with James Prigioni https://www.youtube.com/user/ThePermaculturGarden
6. Self Sufficient Me https://www.youtube.com/user/markyv69
7. The Old Alabama Gardener https://youtu.be/25gV0hSpF1w
8. Garden Tips https://youtu.be/MsxiC-fe_bU
9. https://youtu.be/07pfXEL6gNQ
10. Rick Austin, Secret Garden of Survival Series, paperback
11. Out There, "Wild edibles in the garden," https://youtu.be/vZIwhmatP48
12. Boutenko Films and Books, https://youtu.be/NSxjozvB43Q
13. Outer Spaces, Early Spring Wild Edibles, https://youtu.be/xDmz7bsLlyc
14. Medicinal Plants used by Native Americans on a Daily Basis by Blessed Zone, https://youtu.be/Y8e09BUquB8
15. Motivational Doc Mandela, https://youtu.be/_NNRnsdHM9g
16. Poisonous Plants in your Garden by Blessed Zone, https://youtu.be/0_SGbWCvtnU
17. "How Much to Plant For a Family of Four" (perennially) by Marie Iannoti, thespruce.com
18. Hydroponic Gardening, https://www.thespruce.com/beginners-guide-to-hydroponics-1939215
19. Bill Forstchen, One Second After, Amazon
20. Ruth Stout No Dig, No Water Garden

21. "5 Minute Crafts VS," 27 Gardening Hacks You'll Want to Know https://youtu.be/jD8n2CKEWtA This is a very nicely done video of how to start and propagate plants in simple unique easy ways.
22. Solar Pump
23. Dibbers - Made from a shovel handle with a grip handle about 2' long, shaped to a dull point, with inch markings. I use the butt end of my Father's well oiled grub hoe.
24. Raised garden box plans (3, 4" steel lag screws and decking corner brackets)
25. Tomato poles, bean poles, cucumber lattice and potatoes towers
26. Garden Care the natural way by product and by plants
27. When to Harvest? (Daily all season)
28. Moe's Original Barbecue

At the end of the day milkshakes

STORE CHECKLIST
(Add your items to this list)

- Mulch, potting soil, manure, compost
- Plants and seeds

TO DO LIST

(Add your items to this list)

- Harvest daily
- Mulch
- Pest Control weekly

NOTES

Printed in the United States
By Bookmasters